PRAYERS OF HONORING

GRIEF

Written by Pixie Lighthorse

Lighthorse Publishing, 2018
Redmond, OR

Second Edition

ISBN: 978-0-9982953-2-9

Cover design: Heather Dakota
Layout: Twozdai Hulse

Lighthorse Publishing
SouLodge Ranch, LLC
Redmond, OR 97756
www.pixielighthorse.com

For the brave bonepickers devoted
to celebrating the totality of the lifecycle.

In loving memory of Dove and Willow,
Charlotte and Fox.

CONTENTS

INTRODUCTION

Prayer is a means of connecting to our elevated natures during times of transition. It is during hardship that we can look both deep within and to the cosmic outskirts for guidance and wisdom. Prayer can connect us immediately and intimately to what we feel: What is current, and where the challenges are. It allows us the secure and quiet space to be able to honor what we value.

To honor is to acknowledge and to celebrate. While it may feel counterintuitive to celebrate pain, what you can celebrate is your ability to access your feelings. Your feelings function is a sense not unlike a muscle that asks you to consciously exercise it. The brain is a complex, plastic organ, and it is becoming ever more apparent how it can become hyper-vigilant, triggered by trauma, confused, disorganized, and overwhelmed. To thicken the plot even more, our nervous systems are operating at warp speed, and we are not yet fully equipped with the tools being modern requires in order to navigate through the obstacles of life.

Numbing out feelings due to overwhelm turns them off, and we become accustomed to moving through the world unconsciously, detached and dissociated from them. As natural feelings of suffering and pain are acknowledged, your body will rejoice at its ability to be in the world as it is. The body is a magnificent thing: when its systems come back online, it can bring a feeling of relief as it begins to do its job as nature intended. The task is to create a mindset for the deeper processes to take place.

I owe a deep gratitude to grief. To my mind, grief often appears like a dark and mysterious character in an old mythological novel: draped in black lace—a godmother or midwife taking me on a journey in order to know the full depth of my capacities. These journeys have proven to be fruitful, showing me that I am emotionally much stronger than I give myself credit for.

Grief is a wise elder who needs visitors to their little house out in the wooded countryside away from the rest of humanity. Neglect of their results in missed opportunities to gain understanding and wisdom, just as it does when we fail to sit at the feet of the grandparents to listen. Making the pilgrimage with grief is ultimately strengthening.

Meeting with grief can feel like walking through cobwebs into an alternate world, seeing the bones and the wounds, and bravely offering to tend them. Facing grief asks you to empathize with your pain, the pain of others, and earth's pain, too. Grief deserves your resources, just as fun and joy deserve their place in your vast cosmology of emotions. It is worthwhile to make time and space for sifting through the hurts and healing them.

Strengthening our relationship with grief means making a friend of loss. You may ask, "Why on earth would anyone want to be friendly with the pain of loss?" I suggest it because it is an inevitable part of life, and to be enemies with loss is to reject part of ourselves. The pain of loss is real, and yet we desire to sweep it away and "move on" from it.

We are routinely cultured to "get on with it" from an early age, instructed not to waste time lingering in negativity. When the alternative is avoidance, we actually become more fragile, though we are taught to believe the opposite. Grief remains in the systems of the body, informing our lives in subtle and subversive ways in the form of fear, anxiety, and depression. The whole map of our lives changes when grief is stored away silently. It directs our decisions, impairs or inflates our willingness to take risks, and continues to have its way with us. Toxic, amputated, dishonest, denied, neglected, mutated grief causes disharmony in the body and spirit.

Grief doesn't bite. It is a natural and normal way of dispersing energy through the body's wise and impeccable systems. It is not dangerous unless it is acted out in harmful and neglectful ways. Our thoughts around what grief should look like are the most surprising thing of all. How could it possibly be harmful to be honest about how one is feeling? It is simply the confession of what it was really like then and what it feels like now. It is not the plague of darkness it is made out to be. What a relief!

We humans are vaster than we give ourselves credit for. We must feel the true emotions a circumstance causes to become complete with it. There is no timeline; no way to know what this will look like on the calendar. Completion happens in stages. We know we are healing when we are having more light days than dark. The darkness requires patience and willingness to pan for the golden wisdom of experience. What would it be like if we wore a t-shirt that said, "I am in my healing process" as a reminder to us, and those around us, that we are heavy with the important work of tending grief?

A predominant message we hear and repeat to ourselves is "keep it together." Grief implies falling apart. It does not sound like a process that lends itself to keeping together. Moving feelings through the body creates wellness, like a cleanse. Held in, it becomes stagnant and constipated—a breeding ground for emotional and mental bacteria, thought parasites, and dis-ease.

Simply put, grief is emotional pain caused by loss. The remedy is to keep it moving like a river: talk about it, move your body, write about it, cry it out, hold memorial dinners, honor remembrance dates, eulogize your lost loved ones and unfulfilled dreams, sit by the graves of your abandoned hopes and friendships that have parted ways. Make time to feel the gravity of missed opportunities-—a job you loved, parenting small children, your long-gone menstrual cycle or fertility.

Plan for grief.

Do not become fixated on when you will be finished grieving. Grieve enough. It will let you know if you are complete, not the other way around. You might be asking if it will just go on like this forever. It will not go on forever. It will ebb and flow, weave and bob, disappear for a while and then come back to visit. It may be necessary to confront your boredom and irritability with grief. We mustn't look down on it. It is an essential part of us.

Like those populations in need of our time, empathy, creativity, listening, and resources, grief is treated as a burden. We have no place for it in our modern lives, so we push it to the outer margins hoping we won't have to look at it. As with many important social movements today, looking away is seeming less of an option, and rightfully so. When we learn to be present to the discomfort of pain, more aspects of life will be expanded and honored. It is partly our addiction to anesthetic comforts that has landed us in this collectively difficult place.

It may be that ignoring grief produces a false measure of our ability to persevere through life's challenges. However, it is not the systematic repression of our feelings that makes us graceful, but the ease with which we forgive ourselves and others for being human, making mistakes, and having inconvenient, messy feelings. I do not believe that we are unequipped to grieve, but we seem rather quick to judge when we do allow it. If it prevents our productivity, we resent it. If it stifles a partner's libido, we grow impatient, maybe distant. We have limits around how we handle grief in ourselves and in others. Perhaps we are afraid it will overwhelm us and consume our lives. For this reason, we must learn to grieve our losses when they are happening, and not postpone them until it makes calendar-sense, or until it begins to destroy our health from the inside out. We have to teach ourselves how to manage the emotions that flood and overstimulate our nervous systems.

It is important not to shame or silence those who are grieving something precious that was stolen from them: their dignity, their child, their health, their partner, their home, their safe or secure childhood, their innocence or faith. When you develop patience and wisdom for your own grief, you will find that you have more empathy for others. Often I have heard someone say that they wish another person would "get motivated" and "do something". I wonder if this is not so much a generous desire for the other person's wellbeing as much as a longing to relieve their discomfort with another's suffering or their own untended grief. Perhaps this is because being attentive to another's suffering presents the risk of triggering ours.

See what you can learn by observing yourself witnessing others' grief. It will bring insight about how you are handling your own.

Nothing to grieve, have you? Look around. People are hurting everywhere. The earth is grieving the loss of her biodiversity; humankind is becoming rapidly more unwell due to environmental pollution and economic inequality; governments are undermining freedoms, privacy and liberties; overall mental health is in crisis. We are hooked on the speed of technology and hyper-stimulation. The opportunity to grieve, along with many other feelings, is available to you daily. Keep it moving.

Let it blend seamlessly with your joy. It is not mania to feel deeply disappointed and laugh at the same time. We are deeper containers than we think we are. Make a conscious effort to discover how to hold both at the same time.

In the soup of life are all of the feelings and flavors of our experiences. They swirl together, leaving us gutted about one thing, neutral about some, overjoyed about others. The Mystery holds us, like cradling hands made of stars, like the ladle of the Big Dipper. We can carry the lot of it, right in the same moment. This is because we have the ability to synthesize and honor the totality of life when we become dedicated to being whole.

Grief comes in waves, crashing over us and then subsiding for a time. It hurts... and we can handle pain and suffering. A shamanic approach allows one to broaden the experience of feelings—the invitation is to travel into unknown realms in order to gain understanding and medicine. On the periphery of our single-dimension vision, infinite worlds of multi-dimensions exist. Calling in benevolence and accepting healing energy from the pulse of life helps us move through single-focused suffering and to the other side. By expanding our thinking about the hidden wisdom inside the grief process, we can impose fewer limits on the range of our interaction with, and responses to, our feelings.

Owl is a feminine spirit guide who has helped me through my grief processes. She is a crepuscular creature (neither nocturnal nor diurnal) who surfs the breezes of dawn and dusk, hunting for the mice: symbolic of the little details we miss when we do not look closely. Where our vision is fuzzy, hers is sharp. When we engage the dream states, she is sailing silently over, picking off the shadowy night-roamers, keeping the grounds free of the pestilence and disease of toxic grief. She shows us the healing potential of working together with dreams to discover fears, worries, hopes, and power over adversity. Because untended griefs lie in wait, they can become triggered by other grief in the foreground. Do not be surprised if a riot of "mice" come scurrying out when you say yes to tending the wounds that are most obvious. Maybe Owl will come to you while you are honoring grief work. Thought by some to be a death omen, she has helped me digest my grief whole and release what cannot serve me: the bits that are not nourishing and cannot be turned into clean fuel for living.

Grief is asking to be brought into community conversations again. The death rituals of traditional peoples are examples for us to be led by. Long ago, in my own indigenous lineage, a lost loved one's body was raised up high upon a scaffold and sung back to the Sun for four days and nights. So, too, can we honor our unfulfilled dreams and desires, our missed opportunities for love, and the depths of our pain, both individual and collective. We can lift, sing and pray the lost parts of ourselves back home.

Prayers strengthen our relationship to inner wisdom and our connection to all that exists outside of us. Pray not for yourself to have your grief taken from you, but to learn to hold it, and to be held by the spirits of your ancestors while at the altar. Honor grief by showing up for it. You will find that grief has a way of equalizing all people. Not one of us, even a small child, is without it.

The prayers in this book are designed to flow the reader through the process of grief, not skirt the edges of it with logic or reason. They will take you around the compass so that you have an opportunity to go all the way into the challenges grief presents and come through the other side to honor the wisdom and maturity of actualization. The promise of walking around the wheel of life is to leave no stone unturned where possible. If you miss something, it will invite you right back in when you make the final turn; there will always be opportunities to shed more layers as it goes around and round in a spiral all your living days and beyond.

Imagine that we are in a small boat together. I will do some rowing while you attend the matters that are hurting. These prayers serve to move you gently along in your grief process, but most importantly, they are here to help you understand what is possible when you consent to rise to meet the fullness of your life despite how much it can hurt.

Pixie Lighthorse

FOREWORD

My journey with grief began in smallness and confusion. As a child I felt desperately torn between the deep sorrow and anger of one parent and the controlled denial of the other. Now I understand I was experiencing the polarities of unresolved grief abandoned in a culture that does not know how to contend with loss, betrayal, pain and despair. Children instinctively know there is another way through grief. With no one to listen, they can lose that path. It took the wreckage of my own heartbreak for me to find it again.

Many years later, when I began encountering souls brave enough to share their grief journeys, I was astonished by their willingness to spread out their maps and trace the routes that had led them into the underworld and back. In sacred circles I witnessed their stories, and they witnessed mine. I am forever grateful for those containers of raw truth. They were strong enough to hold the immensity of our grief and transform it, leaving us newborn, vulnerable and somehow incomprehensibly alive.

Staggering about in my darkness, I also found lantern bearers, teachers and wise ones who inhabited the landscape of grief and knew its navigation. This way, they said. Over here, they urged. And I followed. They taught me I was not alone, that the language of grief is universal. They showed me that in community and with ceremony, we can share and release our burdens together.

Pixie and I met in such a place, at a Dagara grief ritual led by Sobonfu Somé in the tradition of her African tribe. We had both journeyed long and hard to be there. Tear-stained, spirits cleansed, we soul-linked in the midst of the release with gratitude and without words. Trust me, you will know those souls when you meet them. They understand there are blessings to be found in the depths, and they are willing to dive for pearls. They will tell you of the sweet strangeness of loss and how it can make the world so achingly beautiful.

Pixie bears her lantern with a brave devotion. She knows grief's terrain and walks its paths with the quiet softness of well-worn shoes. If you have found this book, you have just met a light bearer who can guide you on your journey. No matter how hard the path, how terrible the night, remember there are others out in the storm with you. Call to them, gather them. Open these pages and descend together.

"There is a sacredness in tears. They are not the mark of weakness, but of power. They speak more eloquently than ten thousand tongues. They are the messengers of overwhelming grief, of deep contrition, and of unspeakable love."

~Washington Irving

Jennifer Houston
Founder, The Red Balloon Project

HOW TO USE THIS BOOK

GRIEF is a companion to hold by your heart as you quest inward to honor yourself and what you have been through. It is your humble assistant, serving you and your process of healing and wellness. I have written these prayers to remind you of your connection to something greater than yourself, something that holds you while you are in your healing process.

You have been carrying grief all your life. This book provides an opportunity to honor any pain that you have stuffed down for dealing with at a later, perhaps more convenient time. By holding it in your hands, you have agreed to at least give honoring your pain a try. Your healing is a healing for all. Everyone and everything benefits when a heart's matters are tended.

If confronted by a floodgate that threatens to unhinge all of your waters at once, try writing in a continual stream on the blank and lined pages. Be brave to comfort your fears and hear the voice that reminds you that you will be okay. I believe that grief does not claim lives. Only a lack of grieving builds up and causes implosions and explosions. Grieving does not disable one from feeding the children or tending home, work, and pets. However, any time one is in a healing process, help is appreciated. Know what you need and ask for what you want from those who can help you. Try to be honest about what you are going through. This is how we repair the culture—by valuing what matters and connecting with one another about it.

You may find that you want to set aside a day or a weekend to dedicate to the process of showing up to grief-tending. Planning and undergoing ceremony and ritual may be a way you feel called to embody moving through the process. Honoring loss is not unlike honoring a birthday. Allow it to take up some space in your life.

You may want to find a center or a circle that processes grief in-person or see a healer or therapist to guide you through what you're specifically reconciling. You may want to create a circle of like-minded individuals for processing the kind of grief you are honoring—healing trauma, divorce, death, moving, or life transition.

Address the prayers to anyone or anything that holds you. For some this is the earth, the ocean, or a mountain. For others, it is Jesus, Mother Mary, saints, goddesses, the ancestors. I address my prayers to Great Mystery or Magnificent, while envisioning the bright, energized, hair-like thread of consciousness connecting my life-pulse to all other living things. The most important thing is to do as it serves your tender purpose.

EAST WITH GRIEF

Season: Spring

Element: Air

In the East, big news on the wind is received or remembered, inciting the sting of loss or the memory of suffering. Awareness shines a spotlight on restlessness and aloneness within existence. Here we try to "wrap our heads around" a confusing or disorienting situation.

Challenge: *Overthinking and making brain-sense of emotional terrain.*

Shadow: *Love and loyalty for beginnings has the power to undermine a necessary cycle. Hesitancy to step into the unknown territory of greater consciousness is to be expected but can be frustrating to start and stall as we cling to how things used to be.*

Medicine: *Allow beginnings to be equal in value to endings. Honor that leaving facilitates growth. Enjoy beginnings for what they are best at teaching: presence, willingness to take risks for love, the joy of innocence, and courage to speak dreams out loud. Material dreams are one-dimensional. Strive for understanding of your multidimensionality and the interconnectedness of all things. Allow the mind to hone tools and skills for what is ultimately a soul's lifelong journey to wholeness.*

Keywords for Grief in the East: *youth, enchantment, unmet expectations, disappointment, shock, fear, denial, mourning, invitation, initiation*

Honoring Awareness

Thank you for this transitional day of being part of the mystery.

Thank you for this unexpected information and change of course. Help me overcome my fear of how it will inform my future.

Calm my uneasiness about what is being presented. When I am blindsided, soften my breath, and let me feel its influence on me. During these times, I forget what works well for me. Keep me close to you by bringing my attention to the tension rising in me. Provide a cushion for my rigidity.

Soothe my desire to numb out and activate my miraculous systems for coping. Circulate my blood while I navigate this strange territory. Help me stay open. Help me trust that I can get through this. When I sense that I am contracting, help me lean into trust. Mellow my heart's rhythms when it engages in a race with my thoughts.

When change is threatening to unhinge me, untether me from my illusions of safe harbor. Help me remember that the earth anchors me, that I am equipped to handle what will unfold, that I have seen dissolution before, and made it through.

Ease my need for comfort at the expense of presence. Help me call out to the feelings. Help me navigate this starless nightroad on which I feel so helpless. Help me be with this turn of events roiling in my body and tame my overactive mind.

Turn me toward the mirror so I can accept myself even in desperation. Help me appreciate my form when I cannot get myself together as I believe I am supposed to. Remind me that I can be awake to what is happening and manage fear at the same time.

Inject me with the reminder that I didn't come this far to abandon myself now.

Honoring Confusion

Thank you for this day of circling the drain.

I don't understand what has been presented to me. Release my fixation on finding the gift in it.

Tenderize my refusal of what is in front of me. Tune me into my legs when my heels dig in, so that I notice the domineering pressure of my resistance.

Help me admit when I am likely to deny. Remind me that denial is a critical part of the healing process when I fight what I'm being shown. Let me honor that it is natural to spin in the beginning when nothing makes sense.

Dissolve the haze of fury and help me be patient as the puzzle comes together over time. Show me the events and feelings that have led me into this unwanted cyclone. Show me my part. Show me where I am blaming. Release the shame that I didn't or couldn't make a choice that would have made a difference. Let me gently await clarity, which is sure to come.

Still my mind and calm my overprotective heart. Pause my spinning gears when trying to reverse what I cannot change. Let me slowly ponder the riddle, and let the solving come later.

Place my hands in my lap. Sit me down when I spiral and help me care for myself. Show me your guiding light. Help me create the space I need to take the next step, knowing I can break down the logistics later. For now, just let me inhale and exhale my way through each moment. Teach me to keep breathing through the shock of disbelief.

Receive my fists when they take to the air. Let me struggle and strain until I go limp with surrender. While waiting for a fresher awakening, let me comprehend the lengths I am willing to go.

Honoring Loss of a Loved One

Thank you for this day of profound mourning.

Shroud me in the gloomy garments of bereavement. Drape me in a greying shawl of longing for the one who no longer resides in this world. Make my spirit aware of the transmissions that take place when an earth body becomes light. Help me to honor my person and what they meant to me.

Let me look as shabby as I feel, releasing concerns of what others may think of me. Help me embody the darkness I feel over what has been lost. Show me how to make a ceremony for this occasion.

Help me be present for these feelings in a way that is healing for me. Remind me that it is natural for one big blow to unleash the hoarded sufferings of my past.

Point me to demonstrations of how my people grieved their beloveds for centuries before now. Show me what I can do for my familiars. March me to the mounded graves. Let me make the sacred sounds of this great misery I carry, blood-curdling and guttural.

Help me release my fears about future losses but let me cling to loving life while I am living it. Find me uncrippled by mistrust of nature's divine processes of reclaiming but designate ample space to churn with agitation. When I've lost one I love and I'm on my knees, let me place my agonies at your altar in the woods. Send in the winds to flurry my distress toward the Source.

Let me hold precious the memory of those who have crossed over by letting them be part of me. Ferry my howls across the seas to connect with all those who are aching with loss. Hear our sorrowful voices mingling in one powerful wailing song.

Let the stars absorb my lamentations tonight.

Honoring Loneliness

Thank you for this time to myself to reflect on who I am becoming.

Help me become more tolerant of solitude while preparing to be with others as I am meant to be. It is hard. I crave the company of someone who truly understands and knows me. Help me to perceive that these feelings of desertion will not last forever. Be my friend while I learn to master offering to myself what I have to share with others.

Wade with me into the river but take the stones from my pockets. This is no time for sinking. Baptize me in a sacred ceremony just for me. Help me realize that my challenge is in loving the company I keep when I am alone. Let me rise from within. Let me take this time to lay down my masks and claim my sovereignty.

Help me open my heart to learn the beauty of truth. Teach me to communicate with gentle transparency. Help me to fully inhabit my body and experiences. Lean me into what heals and sustains me—both during my period of peace and quiet, and when the time comes to share my life with another, and then many.

Ease the homesick pang of being orphaned, and direct me toward the places my loving contributions and insights are most needed.

Where I am motherless, let me seek nurture in the right places.

Where I am fatherless, let me find provisions.

Where I am empty, let me permit myself to be filled by your loving current.

When I feel left out, point me to where I belong. Help me end my story of separation.

Help me know what kinds of people make fitting kindreds.

Help me value myself so that I make sound choices in allies.

Honoring Regret

Thank you for this day of acknowledging my mistakes. Thank you for a new lens to see my life through, while feeling the torment of what I am carrying. Thank you for the very palpable anguish and remorse I am able to endure. Help me reconcile my errors.

There are many things I would do differently if I could. Help me reach out to those I have wronged. I know how to make amends. Show me how to forgive myself. Help me restore balance to my soul so that I can step solidly forward. For those I have had to part ways with, let me be kind in my thoughts toward both of us. Resolve me to a daily decision to be responsible for my actions should our paths cross again.

Help me release my belief that I am foolish. Replace my shame with devotion to loving from a stronger version of my heart. When I stumble again, which I will, help me find my sure-footedness and release old stories that harm my maturation and fulfillment.

Help me understand what was at work when I mishandled myself, especially if there was a wounded part of me acting out my pain. Route me toward the education that will help me understand my intricate relationship to what still hurts. Show me how to brave the growing process, so that I know how to make assessments and correct my thinking when I miscalculate.

Humble me and help me become able to live with my humanness. Help me to allow my mistakes and others theirs. Subdue my overactive need to control outcomes.

Release my need to punish and over-correct and help me let go of any part of me that believes there is only one chance.

Germinate in me a seed of accountability while helping me manage the jungle of my day-to-day missteps.

Honoring Insecurity

Thank you for this day of total surrender. There are many things I'm uncomfortable with, but few are as devastating as losing what helps me to feel secure. I have heard I am my own home, but today I feel particularly disconnected.

When I am adrift, let the constellations be my guides. When I need shelter, let me become proficient at building. When I need protection, show me how to weave a shirt for my back. When I am hungry, guide me to be the provider of my nourishment. When I am slighted, let my defense be curiosity. When I am attacked, let my shield be the light you surround me with. When I have been taken from, let me seek ways to stabilize and replenish.

Remind me that when I feel powerless, I have my original relationship with all life. I am one part of the infinite and interconnected web of earthbound beings.

Teach me sensible ways to free myself from danger, sabotage, and threat. Help me to be sound when I am tempted to crumple into a heap. Remind me to source myself in times of doubt. When I am depleted, let me fortify my reserves with all the rest I can give myself.

Be the brace that supports me when I feel wobbly—when I cannot remember the tools, I already possess that help me endure the unknown. Let me stand solid on the earth while I gather the courage to be on this shifting ground.

Help me dig deeper within for steady supplies of power that are real and lasting.

Honoring the Loss of a Dream

Thank you for this day of cradling my deep disappointment. I'm torn to pieces about not achieving the results I was seeking, despite my persistent efforts. Temper my insatiable need to understand why it worked out this way. Steer me away from patterns of believing that I just can't get it right.

Help me manage the sinking feeling that extraordinary things will not happen for me. Show me the medicine. Soothe me as I feel the inconsolable longing, I carry for the life I'm not allowed to live at this time. Release me from the complicated grip of self-blame and blame of others who had a hand in this.

While I am bargaining with all my might to breathe life into what cannot be, let me rebirth myself into a container that can hold my grief. Can there be any freedom in a different path? Can I pause long enough to hear your instructions? Be the voice that says I can take all the time I need to move through this substantial setback.

Help me contend with my desire to force a different outcome. Mature my perspective about my path heading in a direction I wouldn't choose if it were only up to me. Show me what I can do with this experience that will be fruitful. If I can't spin it into gold, let me use it for the higher good of my heart, and serve other hearts, too.

Help me conjure the energy for allowing the unknown architecture to be revealed for what I am supposed to be doing. Summon inside of me a purpose greater than the one I had imagined for myself.

JOURNAL PROMPTS FOR THE EAST

Is there a part of me that is rejecting the present in favor of what once was?

Do I value the thrill of beginnings over middles and endings?

Can I bear the anxiety of new changes while staying open and vulnerable?

Can I sit still without desperately seeking solutions?

What rituals and ceremonies will honor what I've been through?

How might I connect with what I loved about the past without becoming stuck?

What will it take to forgive myself? Who am I still blaming and punishing?

What helps me know I am built for life and grow stronger through its challenges and hardships?

How can I source a sense of belonging when I feel alone?

Who are my models for stable, sustainable growth in my world?

How can I become steady during rocky periods?

SOUTH WITH GRIEF

Season: Summer

Element: Fire

The fire of South fuels movement over hurdles like a champion dressage horse. However, grief is not a sporting event. It is a gradual process of cleaning the wounds with care. In the South, healing can be interrupted by attempting to move too quickly or supported by bringing intention and attention to managing your energy supply.

Challenge: *Staying connected to yourself, restoring energy, and patiently allowing the grief experience to unfold and reveal your depths.*

Shadow: *Overdoing it, burnout. Zealous creative energy overpowers grief, while disappointment over unmet expectations becomes consuming. It is not uncommon in the South to buy every book, attend every class, and attempt to make logical sense of an intuitive and emotional process.*

Medicine: *Allow warm passion for life to animate intimacy with others as it becomes feasible to express. Gathering by the hearth results in closeness and love, which eventually hurts to lose. Develop compassion and empathy for yourself as you establish yourself as one who walks toward love knowing what is at risk. Seek vitality and community among those grieving similar losses.*

Keywords for Grief in the South: *yearning, reality, difficulty, community, endurance, logistics, processing, logic, movement, expression*

Honoring Paralysis

Thank you for this day of frozen stillness. Hold me while I'm in this cocoon of difficulty. When I feel stuck, let me allow myself to be held—to relax into the ample arms of the void.

Help me find the filament that connects me to the sacred, geometric, intelligent cosmos find me. Remind me that I am not grasping for anything but the knowledge that I am connected. Show me no false rafts to keep me afloat. Let me sense what I know but cannot see. Let the invisible slowly become visible. Remind me that I pulse with the electricity of life even when dormant.

Drain my frustrations, which cause me to spin my gears and wear me out. Mute the ceaseless chatter in my mind that urges me to do something, anything. The doing can wait. Let this still state be a healing place, if only temporary. Help me trust that I will know when and how to move. Help me reassure my mind with ample space to be in this chrysalis, becoming soundless in order to hear the sparks of the fire that can warm me into the form of my higher spirit.

When I feel emotionally flattened, infuse me with the fragrant beauty sniffed on a forest floor. When I feel dull and listless, let me move tectonically to care for myself without the urge to do more. When I feel fastened to my nest or ashamed about loitering, blanket me with honesty about how patient a process this is. Let the cemented weights on me bring deeper commitment to the art of slowing down.

Keep me connected, knowing that tranquility grows inside of me and is a good enough place to be for now. Help me amplify my access to the glowing forces that brought me here.

Honoring Shelter

Thank you for this day of signing off. Today I cannot meet anyone's expectations. Thank you for the wisdom to know it is okay for me to claim a gap of spaciousness between me and the world.

Help me to detangle the nerves coating the outside of my skin. Remove my need to be available to others at the cost of myself. Shelter me from unwanted rays. I know that I cannot linger here forever, but I need this day to be accountable to myself and reinstate my open-heartedness. Place me inside a calcified shell and house me in waveless, windless lodging.

Guide my hands to create a protective haven that allows me to nurture my body and emotions. Help me build a temporary umbrella like this when I need to get away from the turbulent storm that frays my spirit. Heighten my awareness that I can come here, so that I enter and depart consciously, not reflexively or out of fear. Remind me to disclose to those who care about me that I'm intentionally going in for respite, and to ask them to hold me accountable to meet my agreements to come out into the sun. Remind me that it is curative to come and go for self-treatment.

Remind me that it is okay to seek solace from the clatter, but to be sure to strengthen myself through this practice. Aid me in the process of not becoming more fragile for life on the outside. Show me the techniques for listening to my evolution. Clear away the rubbish of my wounded mind that says I am not suited for life outside my hideaway.

Help me use my time in this sacred place well, focusing my attention on the creative energies I need in order to pour the warm oil of right medicine on my fretfulness.

Honoring Yearning

Thank you for this day of piercing desire for things to be different. Teach me to be with what actually is. Help me to accept that my appetite to move beyond is my body's way of writhing through the discomfort of difficulty. Help me to realize that I will get there if I meet my present grief and those that lie underneath it. Help me to honor the intrinsic function that is helping me slowly begin to understand the depth of my suffering, and its power over me.

Help me comprehend that craving is my teacher. Show me the child inside of me who was not filled in the way I needed to be. Help me to be free of obligation to my trauma and put me on the road of giving myself care in the way I need most. Show me that I can count on myself now.

Nurture my heart, my womb, and my broken body. Lay the hands of your Light on my discontentedness. Fill me up with the beauty of each moment of presence, even when my cup seems to overflow with sadness. Let me hold it all. Balance my longing for tears with my longing for laughter. Make room for both of them inside of me.

Let me work with you until I am absolutely certain it will not always be this way, and let's continue our collaboration. Help me transform my belief that my destiny is to feel empty and distraught. Remind me to make meaning of my world by being meaningful in the world—by sharing my song of misfortune with others and punctuating it with what has helped me most.

Teach me to be satisfied with the quality of my real emotions. When light and dark live inside me in equal measure, neither will consume me.

Honoring Unwellness

Today I feel like hell. Help me as I tangle with the state of disease that is eroding my sanity and serenity. Help me hold on with a soft but sure grip. Help me regenerate my healthy cells by connecting my mind to the parts of my body asking for attention and discovery. I can lay my angst down on this dark altar.

I know I'm often asking you for a miracle here. The real marvel might be for me to allow myself to feel the depth of my sorrow about my health. When I am able, help me be an advocate for those who suffer. Connect me to others so that I do not isolate. Let us support one another. Help me see the medicine in my vulnerability and brokenness. Engage my filter for discerning snake oil from salve.

Help me be with my sorrow, and not dismiss myself because I'm not measuring up in the way I think I should. I have missed out on a lot of life due to obstacles in my body, and this is at times heartbreaking. Help me give back to myself what I have been robbed of. Help me to make new grooves in my brain when it is focused only on the familiar sensations of pain.

Strengthen me to be with discomfort without being its prisoner. Let me make good use of my downtime, by recognizing when it is time for battle and for recovery. Fill my tissues and organs with your light, help my mind settle, and let me trust it. Help me find the clear pathways toward which to direct my steps.

Help me dedicate to inner excavation, while growing my network of dependable external resources. Help me be my own ally and not my enemy.

When my physical systems falter, make my spirit strong and ready for renewal.

Honoring Loss of Control

Thank you for this exhausting day of pure chaos.

May I seek to loosen my stranglehold on what I cannot ultimately keep together, so that deeper understanding of what is at work can flow in. May I dedicate myself to becoming more at ease with all that is flowering in directions I cannot stop. Help me to see where I can be useful and focus my energies there. Reinforce my awareness that I can do my part for evolvement rather than striving unceasingly for perfection.

Help me see control as the illusion of containing what is not mine to hold. Let me fall apart when I need to, and make room for others to splinter into smithereens, too. Let there be a return to wholeness that offers more than can be found in a tight, anxious cluster. Let me make space for more possibilities to unfold, not just the one I hope for. Help me to see where I habitually strive for control, but don't actually want to be in charge. Let the sword I carry be swung only at false perceptions.

Open me to the real experience of life, free from the need to sweep up around it obsessively. Help me take care of the cluttered rooms in my mind, flushing out the build-up of reflexive patterns that no longer serve me.

Help me cope with unpredictable circumstances and environments, knowing that I will find the tools to buffer my hyper-responsiveness. Help me learn to let go. Guide my nerves to sanctuary when I quicken to overreact.

Inspire me to delight in emancipation from the confinement of my ideologies of supreme exactness. Unshackle me from rigid expectations and smooth my brow with the hush of my appreciation of you.

Honoring a Broken Heart

Thank you for the strength to walk the dog and feed the children on this day of feeling snapped and fractured.

Help me rewrite the story that my heart is made solidly of scar tissue and can bear no more wounding. Remind me of the times when I believed I could withstand no more, only to find that you made me willing to love and risk trusting again. Help me understand the infinite capacity for love inside of me, which will last beyond my body's time here on earth. Teach me of the heart's regenerative nature, of its extraordinary ability to heal itself without outside help. Urge that this one is an inside job, that it knows how to rise from ashes.

Teach me of the spiritual anatomy of the human heart, enable me to trace its topography with my senses and uncover the mysteries of how I love. Let me visit ground zero with offerings of tribute for how my heart was able to grow wings. Don't allow me to clip them out of fear.

Help me feel each raw edge, every splintered fragment, and torn fiber. Teach me not to count them or injure myself further because of them. Help me sculpt the shrapnel of unmet expectations into a strong shape that will love and be loved well.

Allow me to take generous time to make peace with the searing ache of loss, betrayal, and abandonment. When the pain is excruciating, let me cross my arms over my heart to embrace my center. When the lights dim and the familiar shades come down, let me bathe myself in cleansing sobs.

Remind me that the heart's purpose is to deliver oxygen to the sacred waters that flow through me, and put my focus on the stewardship of my body and spirit.

Honoring Vigil

Thank you for this day of carrying the candles for what is no longer manifest. Thank you for the nocturnal time and space for loving in this brilliant and connected way. Thank you for the opportunity to deliver the fragrant blooms of life to that which has passed. Guide my hands to source mementos of beauty to honor what was and give me the strength to carry a heart full of homage to the remembrance.

Unbury my pain. Discharge the sorrows that come forth. Thaw my consciousness, so that I may feel the swell even of long-held, untended sufferings. Let me take ownership of them. I will be shown many ways to numb out by those who value avoidance. Reveal to me the blessings of being a creature who can feel. Help me see grief as a ceremony of remembering meant to help me move the feelings up, out, and through my body.

Help me remember the purpose of honoring grief and not be tempted to make a tidy event of it. Weave ribbons around those present, making kindred spirits of all of us who pledge to keep the memories alive.

Help me face the disappointment of loss with the passion of raw presence. Let me see that this body is made stronger by the emotions I fear will break me down. Reframe my perspective about "breakdowns," so that my mind can support my body's unique potential for healing itself. Remind me that ash is a potent fertilizer.

Demonstrate how feeling charges me, how smoke shifts effortlessly like water, and how the light that burns up the day must eventually give way to the reflective solace of the moon. Remind me that endings are actually beginnings—that when the candles go out and flowers fade, the real work commences.

JOURNAL PROMPTS FOR THE SOUTH

What do I wish to avoid feeling?

Can I appreciate that my systems are specifically designed to recover and heal from injury?

In what ways might my injuries bring me more to life?

How can I move my body in ways that express what I am feeling?

How is paralysis my teacher? Frustration my thermometer? Stillness my echolocation device?

How can I be transparent about the armor I'm wearing and conscious about its effects on my loved ones?

How can I stop blaming myself and others?

What will it take to forgive myself? What will be required for me to forgive others? Where am I unwilling or unable to forgive?

How can I reorganize my thoughts in order to align with my sphere of control? When my best laid plans don't work out, how might I react differently?

How can I show up as a steward to my body and spirit?

WEST WITH GRIEF

Season: Autumn

Element: Water

The West invites inward healing. It is often passed over in hurried attempts to sidestep the pain of messy hardships. Here lies the repository for the pieces and parts that we have no time for. It is the graveyard at the crossroads where grief work thrives. Travel into the underworld to desegregate rejected aspects.

Challenge: *Facing ghosts and skeletons in order to gather dissociated fragments and integrate the abandoned contents of the soul.*

Shadow: *When submerged in the dark pool of processing raw feelings, we become aware enough to be responsible in communication, behavior, and action. It can be tempting to isolate or ride the energy downward. The cauldron of deserted contents bubbles up in the depths of the soul causing a ghastly and heavy fatigue.*

Medicine: *Saltwater cleanses wounds without blame, scapegoating, and misdirection of pain. Leave behind vengeful, victimy attitudes in favor of synthesizing the totality of your experiences without being defined by judgement. Choose raw emotion over false identifications.*

Keywords for Grief in the West: *maturity, adulting, cleansing, inward, dark, flow, shadow, floodgates, release*

Honoring Trauma

Thank you for this day of seeking to understand what happened inside of me when I was sliced to the bone swiftly, as well as worn down slowly.

Show me how my experience diminished me. Let me attend the consequences of having my systems mishandled. Unveil what the experience taught me and is teaching me. Reveal with clarity the knowledge and empathy that came of it, without need for appreciations. Remind me of how I have adjusted in the wake, and how I can connect to my original nature.

Help me recognize the mystifying glue that has held me together all these years. What is it within me that allows me to still be animated by your fine and wild, subtle electrical current? Help me intermingle my theories with yours about what kept me going.

How has my survival shown me the tenacity of my spirit, which finds me panting with passion? What am I being prepared for? Am I infinitely stronger than I think I am? Show me how I have stayed in league with life, and how to build on my inner force. Open me to reception of your transmissions about how my traumas are still affecting me. Make me a clear vessel of keen awareness.

Let me join with others who have pulled through to celebrate our resilience. Let me see that all of humankind is suffering and that my voice and story are valuable pieces for the collective.

Help me develop tools for coping with the memory of the events, while steering myself into the present moment and the very different circumstances I'm creating for myself.

Let my breath be my reminder that I made it through, and my heartbeat the drum that subdues all interference as I tune into my static-free channel of truth and healing.

Honoring Lowlands

Thank you for these dark, still, halcyon days to contemplate the meaning of life's confusing dilemmas and losses. Help me with this heavy, clouded walk. Help me to realize that I can make profound meaning of my time spent underneath the weighted blanket.

Help me know what to do with the blessing and curse of feeling everything. I cannot turn off my responsive methods of perceiving. Help me to be with myself without believing I

am defective or must put on a mask to go out. Channel my efforts to contend with this level of intensity in a society unreceptive to those who feel so much. Help me be one who creates safe spaces while looking for the disenchanted pieces of my soul.

Help me sort truth from falsehood skillfully. Help me to see that my time spent below contains useful nuggets for life above. Train me to be confident, knowing that what I bring back from the places many dare not go is treasure. Let my days in the underworld be a safe and fruitful place to cultivate poise. Help me orchestrate my thoughts for eloquent expression.

When I am down the well, sifting through the repository of shadows, and wondering what fresh hell this existence will serve up next, help me to remember that I dredge the lake for myself and all of humanity. Remind me that my affinity for depth is a gift that isn't totally understood yet. Help me want to be here and keep my sense of humor. Point me to others who are having a layover here, as well.

Allow me to tour the spectrum of swampy marshes within, exploring moss-draped secrets and mysterious remorses in order to surface with gems that satisfy my deep-diving, soul-searching nature.

Honoring Isolation

Thank you for this day of removing myself from the presence of others. Thank you for aloneness and the strength to be with myself. Make me cognizant of when I need to take space from others, so that I do not retreat in an abandoning way. Help me to know my needs so I can plan my departure and re-entry.

Help me to sequester myself away from the bustle of activity, so I may begin to understand how my systems are growing and shifting. Insulate me from the noise of the outside world. Let me learn to be a master of my own energy. Help me skillfully turn on and turn off in ways that allow me to be at peace, and also real with myself.

When I become miserable or afraid, remind me to enjoy my own company. Seat me by the bonfire of my heart beside the crashing waves, so that my alone time is introspective, healing, and reflective. Show me how my reserves are built and restored in a practice of solitude and meditation. Cultivate in me a respect for my ways and how I relate to you. Let me remember how water becomes still by being left alone.

When a friend bids me farewell, deter my wounded judgment. Bring me to the threshold of acceptance for paths that part. Help me feel the gravity of the empty space and breathe fully into it.

When obstacles arise to greet me, let me meet them eye-to-eye, unlimited in my willingness to chart my moves. Where my thoughts and feelings are complicated, let me not fixate on the complexity but surrender and be bound vigorously to life.

Help me recognize how I have been fragmented. Be the basket in which I gather the lost pieces of myself.

Honoring Tears

Thank you for this weepy day of letting it all out. Open up my sacred waterways and let me celebrate the wide river of empathy for myself and all who suffer. Flow with me as I row my way through what wants to be released from behind the dam.

Wash my wounds and tumble me until my ragged edges are smooth. Remind me of the infinite bounty of compassion and love I can bring to myself when I am hurting. Whisper reminders that tears are a detoxifying gift for my body and earth's body, too. Let me treasure each one like a diamond formed from the coal of my sorrows.

The salty waters in me are just as your oceans: The birthplace of all life, a reminder of home. Holy smokes, I have been so afraid of crying myself dry. What a blessing that these saline fluids can reconstitute my brittle spirit. May my tears be a thanksgiving for all life, both on earth and in the seas, which suffers from humanity's rapid progress, shortsightedness, and neglect. Let me weep for the parched pain of indifference and ambivalence to violence.

Thank you for not making me of stone and for removing my stoicism. Let me courageously throw open the vaults of what I have forgotten that I bear. Help me stir the dormant, slimy mud creatures within and invoke the banshee cries of loss. Take away my fear that sorrow held down will turn on me and remind me that my grievances are due to come out so my body may be refreshed.

Lift my intonations to the Sky Nation to reverberate for my soul and the collective soul of humankind. Let me wail the stagnancies clear with the vibration of my miraculous pipes.

Honoring Coping

Thank you for this day of remembering my tools. On days when I am forgetful and in pain, let me become still enough to summon them into my hands and heart. Fortify my knowledge that amnesia and anesthesia do not allow me to stay in flow—that they are the great and silent burdens that clog and complicate my life. Help me stage my own resistance, confront my obstacles, and compose the voices within me that build resilience.

Thank you for every breath, stretch, moment of outreach, and help line. Thank you for spaciousness, patience, and all that I've gathered to manage my emotions. Thank you for the people who will listen while I am feeling around in the dark.

Let me value the process of growing my resources for grappling with the challenges life rolls toward me. Eliminate my thought that I can't handle one more thing. Remove my malignant, shame-filled thought patterns that find me stuck in loops, deeming my losses not worthy of my attention. When I am centering my whole focus on the sharp and unjust bite of injury, let me relentlessly re-visualize the headquarters where signals and transmissions are taking place. Remind me that fear of pain leads to tension, and tension leads to pain.

Help me become graceful about respecting my states of being.

Help me to notice when it is time to tend and cleanse and create space for myself.

Help me to under-commit and under-schedule myself, while developing new strategies for survival.

Show me how to take intensive care of myself rather than exhausting my energy in an attempt to meet trivial demands.

When I think I'm at the end of my rope, remind me that I am the rope, and what frays me is overvaluing superficial, convenient responses to my deep interior experience.

Honoring Transmutation

Thank you for helping me see my broken pieces as beautiful and worthy. Thank you for helping me lay into the earth what has become oppressive on my soul, and for helping me see the importance in my courage to feel.

Scrub my body, heart, and mind of their accumulated stresses and unaddressed anguish. Let me stop the abuses and misfortunes from telling my future. Help me author my personal story of strength and perseverance while ripening me for rebirth. Let me strip off unwanted debris with my hands and behold how feasible it is for me to move my own energy.

Help me see my offerings like fallen leaves that nourish the bustling, hungry communities of unseen beneficials living below the surface. Let the intensity of the weight I've been carrying feed the soil of my spirit. Help me plant the seeds of tomorrow's wellness and water them with my tears. Let every creaking wail of sorrow be an investment in the freedom of tomorrow.

When my griefs begin to release, let me feel the lightening of my heart like a dandelion setting free its seed-wishes. Let these composted traumas and hopes for the future quell my desire for an endless summer. Cover them gently in preparation for nature's season of reflection and restoration.

Open me to recurrent occasions of self-cleaning for giving my spirit, body, and mind the precious attention it is asking for. Make me an enthusiastic gardener for my well-being. Fill me with willingness to allow downtime when I have done what I can do for now.

I trust you to finish the job in my dreams while I rest.

Honoring Healing

Thank you for bathing my wounds in the patient salve of consciousness. Thank you for helping me rise to float weightless on your promise of light. Thank you for the invisible thread that connects me to you.

I have known some suffering. Help me see the dark woods not as something to hurry out of but find grace and wisdom in traveling willingly to and from. I am grateful for all of

the ways I've been guided. Thank you for helping me tune into my internal navigation system when I am lost. Help my private lantern of presence glow with the gritty fuel of overcoming.

Let me not seek to escape from what is asking for my attention and love. Help me identify the gifts of relief in my healing process and integrate them into my being. Show me how to be irrepressible.

Help me work with the potency of my memories, so that when grief pulls at me, I respond with compassion. Do not let me be a deserter, leaving essential parts of my miraculous being high and dry. Call me back again and again when I forget what I have learned and attempt to bolt.

I am grateful to know how exquisitely I have been made to feel and heal. Thank you for showing me that grief will not kill me, that my sorrows are not toxic—that only an obstinate will to hoard them secretly presents a problem. Teach me to grieve my losses in the moment, until I am complete. It is okay if it takes a lifetime to sense that my house is in order. Help me have the courage to claim a different shape for my life than history foretold.

Refresh my spirit with the waters of nature. Give me language to communicate my experience with others who are on a path of mending.

JOURNAL PROMPTS FOR THE WEST

Where in my body am I carrying fear of healing my sorrows?

What can I offer myself that will help me be in healing process and fulfill my daily duties?

What steps can I take to dissolve the crystallized build-up that is calcifying my relationship to my vitality?

What offerings might I place on an altar to connect me to my ancestors, and to the healing my lineage needs?

What caused me to have to ignore my pain and can I be strong to face it now?

What's in it for me to continue telling a story that weighs me down and holds me back?

Who can help me when I need to get my feelings up and out?

How can I express my grief in the moment or shortly after it arises in me?

What strategies must I implement to keep myself safe when I am being pulled in by false ideas about myself or my pain?

How were darker emotions handled in my family of origin?

What was traumatic for me that I have been minimizing?

NORTH WITH GRIEF

Season: Winter

Element: Earth

Earthy North integrates wisdom by traveling through the minefields of the abandoned parts of the psyche, synthesizing and strengthening the soul. Experiences, ideas, passions, and regrets are alchemized into sophisticated intelligence and understanding. By honoring the pain of loss and undertaking the task of grieving, we take responsibility for our humanness.

Challenge: *The pull to rush back into the East or South to relieve the discomfort of the healing process with thinking and doing.*

Shadow: *Impatience for results stuffs pain back down, sending the message that you are not built for the whole journey of life. Sedentariness or paralysis is not the same as becoming still and appreciative. It is easier to dismiss or medicate the simple beauty of your exquisite nature*

Medicine: *Allow the earth to hold and ground you for a full cycle or season. Engage in life review. Meditate while the work is done inside of you and in your dreams. Prioritize sleep, trust and recovery. Stillness helps body wisdom rise to the top of the mind while the world waits for your return. Finish what you started.*

Keywords for Grief in the North: *application, stillness, acceptance, ceremony, ritual, community, outreach, essence, dignity, resilience, gratitude*

Honoring Acceptance

Thank you for this day of sitting bravely with what has moved through me.

Help me agree to cooperate with the past. I am receptive to what comes next. Give me the green light to settle into my new way of being with this version of my pain. I will not oppose or fight against what comes my way but commit to reverence of my innate ability to heal. Help me resolve and diffuse my reactions to what still haunts me. Keep me honest about what I have worked through and what continues to require love and attention.

Remind me that resolution does not mean that I will not feel my scars tingling with the memory of what happened. Magnify my ability to legitimize what hurt me. Tune me into the truth that suffering doesn't go away completely, for me or anyone else. Bring peace to my jagged edges with each admission of what is real for me—and for all.

Teach me to respect my right to feel without blaming others. Help me stand up for my feelings so they do not become an avalanche again. I consent to honor myself with frequent tributes, awareness, clarity, and check-ins. Help me create the space that I need in order to be with all aspects of myself.

Remind me not to stash pain away or hide it in shame. Help me wear my medals openly and collaborate with the persistent effects of suffering. Help me to reshape my being according to who I am in my heart, and always have been.

Help me opt for authenticity and integrity over convenience and the power of old fears.

Honoring Relief

Thank you for the gift of release and reprieve from carrying an antiquated, heavy load. Help me acknowledge and honor what has been living inside of me, so that I may become lighter and more in tune with nature. Where woe remains, let me build a nest of patience around it. I am willing to make generous space for what is still present.

Thank you for helping me acknowledge the scratchy year-round coat I've been wearing. I'm in awe of what respite feels like to my weary soul. Help me welcome vulnerability when splintered hurts pile up, and I am tempted to close off and run away.

Remove my judgment about this necessary progression through tending stillness. Help me to see that I require space away from criticism to reset my barometers. Let me also become sturdier with the knowledge that other's reactions to my healing process are not my business.

Help me remember how unpacking my pieces of ancient luggage alleviates daily stress and decreases the pressure I put on myself to always have it together. Remind me that grieving is a balm from the ancestors that lets me be kind to myself. Allow me to bless the people in my life with the compassion I have learned to give myself. Connect me again and again to the tapestry of life by my sacred thread of consciousness and attention to my life-force.

Teach me to put tending my garden of griefs at the top of my list and earth my intentions to walk a path that honors strength through perseverance. Let me share my tales of overcoming the worst parts of re-sculpting my reality to match my intentions for my life.

Honoring Earth

Thank you for this day of celebrating the sacred ground that supports me. Help me be a voice for the pain I carry about what is devastating our home. Help me to understand that earth-body grief is agonizing. Help me look to her as a mirror for what is happening inside each of us and manifesting outwardly.

Soothe my suffering and dismay about the heartbreaking news of what is happening to Earth. Ease my fears that for-profit pillaging and ruthless gutting will not soon come to an end. Help me realize that my healing and ability to work with my grief will help Earth heal, too—that as I grow my compassion for what is real for me, I will continue to expand my capacity for compassionate treatment of the planet.

Let me give constructive consult to those I blame for the state Earth is in.

Let me reduce what I collect.

Let me be a cleaner where I walk.

Let me dream visions of how to be of service to her when I sleep.

Let the reasons I care be my true north.

Help me partner with, rather than use, Earth's resources. Let every day be one in which I value the soil, the plants, the stones, the Standing Ones who bear fruit that feeds me, and the wild creatures. Help me bring all of my available efforts to appreciating and learning about Earth's life-giving waters and how to protect them.

Align me with those who are making changes in spite of their despair. Let me offer myself in stewardship to the Mother who needs my support. Help me restore my natural resources so that I may be a beneficial organism here and inspire those around me to treat our home lovingly.

Honoring Essence

Thank you for the indispensable qualities I am learning to love about myself as I allow myself to heal. Help me remember that feeling needn't compete with my being and doing states. Help me to cherish who I am as One Who Feels. Prevent me from using my sensitivity to shield myself from others.

Who am I without the pollution of my disregarded injuries? Help me find out what is under all of this protective armor. Lead me to everything that will help me discover the sacred nature of my potentiality.

Help me strengthen my competence by keeping my system in good working order. Repeat in me the need to flush my wounds and seek right medicine. I am open to honoring and receiving help from unseen sources. Help me value virtues unassociated with my vocation. Help me know myself for more than what the world applauds me for. Help me identify as one with an unmasked heart. Uncloak my most passionate desires to love life.

When the allure of returning to old ways of stuffing and stashing appear, let me think of my body as a canyon containing the river I hold most dear. Remind me of its need to flow freely and not become dammed up. Let me imagine my river being honored fully, sparkling and clear, apparent with geologic evidence of what has happened, and uncontaminated by the debris of neglect.

Emphasize transparency in my thinking, responsibility in my actions, and translucence in my being. Distill my ideas to bring about greater understanding for humanity and regard for precious life.

Concentrate my unique talents and help me put them to good use.

Honoring Experience

Thank you for this day to reflect on where I've been and how it matters. Thank you for maturing me to the point of releasing my concern for outward appearances. Thank you for the opportunity to come face-to-face with what was feasting on my serenity. Thank you for freedom from old identities and worn out ideas of myself. Thank you for the trials and evolutions that brought me into this form. Help me find the beauty in it without straining and going off path.

Help me hold my former trials up to the light for closer examination. Help me see my ordeals as backcountry trails that have brought me through to the other side. Help me notice that I am here in my body, with Earth beneath me and Sky above me. Suspend me in the present moment to accept where I sit still, awaiting further instructions from the cosmic source of inspiration that I have become so fond of dialoguing with.

When the luster of youth wears away and I grasp clumsily backward for good old days, deliver me back to right now, the only place I fit and belong. Help me release my illusions about the past being superior to the present. Let me audaciously say goodbye to what has become complete with an ecstatic dance from the top of the mountain I have climbed.

Let me be a beacon for others by telling the hardy myths of survival. Help me to bring purpose and significance to the fresh narrative I am living.

Honoring the Dream World

Thank you for helping my soul travel into the outer realms to gather intelligence about what my deep Self will continue to ponder and work through. Thank you for the guides and messengers who show up to help me understand where I am afraid and worried.

When I can't make sense of what is coming up for me, help me turn to my dreams for reliable transmissions. Let me make offerings to the guardians of my sleep-time so that my visions are clear. Let me gather the plants that protect and inspire pathways for new perspectives. Let me bundle them tenderly and place them under my pillow.

Connect me to the influence of the shining moon. Take me on the long soul walks with her that alter my relationship to time. Help me see that my productiveness on this journey is supported by the strength I gather through restfulness and pause.

Help me decode the riddles and collect the symbols that affirm my healing. Provide me with unlocked passage into my beautiful mind that makes movies from what I am unconsciously designating real estate to. Train me to trust what I see and acknowledge that I may sometimes be disguised as each character that shows up in the landscape. Hone my discernment for helpful interpretation. Help me multiply my gratefulness for the ambassadors who have influenced me and visit me in the dream world carrying a message about tending my soul.

Power me down to unwind in the darkness, so I can power up to live in full-color during my days.

Honoring Ceremony

Thank you for the song of sorrow I have carried over the long road to the graves of my dead. Make me unafraid to call them out loud by name. Let me retain my private chant in the well of my memory and recall it when grief visits me. Elevate my voice until it reverberates with resonance, the sensational flow of life-force I unconsciously denied myself. Lift my incantation up to the Sky Nation as a gift. Send it beneath the loamy Earth Mother to direct, nourish, and protect all I have left behind.

Move my feet to the dance that is drumming the rhythm of our hearts into the earth, loosening the dense, compressed crust to encourage awakening. Let me climb to the top of the ruins to shake free the remains of the past in order to bear hug my future.

Guide my hands to prepare a rainbow feast on a table set with the silver of gratitude. Be the flames that light the unending rows of candles illuminating the banquet of outpouring. Place a golden urn at my strong and vulnerable center that flashes with the appreciation of knowing myself through and over my intimate obstacles.

Let me know my spirit in the ways you do. Allow me to hear the name you call me. When I feel lionhearted, let me allow others to know the depths of where I've been. Make me a bold memoirist who brings flower crowns to all that I honor through full cycles of growth and transition. Place me on the back of the mythological beast that will carry me the rest of the way.

Make me narrow at the top and broad at the base so I may be a clear channel to send these prayers up as I walk the spiral labyrinth with intention for all my days to come.

JOURNAL PROMPTS FOR THE NORTH

How can I honor what I have been through?

How can I allow my heart to rest when pain does not subside?

What does resolution of grief look like to me?

What is the benefit of sitting still with the pain of loss?

How can I create sacred space in which to grieve?

What can I include in a ceremony to honor my griefs?

What can I no longer afford to look away from that feasts on my serenity?

How can I bring more patience to the unfolding of my true nature?

How can I work with my dreams to reinforce my relationship to life?

What is the essence of me that pain and suffering have not changed?

How might I talk about my healing process and unmasking my grief?

AFTERWORD

Grieving is not work for the weak-spirited. Time calls us to face the traumas and discomforts of loss when it is necessary for moving forward. This is perhaps why a deep frustration is felt when revisiting pain that holds us back. It is experienced in layers.

The Medicine Wheel challenge is that the journey spirals around and around through time, space, maturity, and changes. We experience each new day in the East at sunrise, completing it in the evening in the North. We also greet the East at the beginning of life and complete it in the North at the inevitable end. We circle it within a calendar year and within each season of life. In this way, many gears turn at once. The folds of time open up for us with each initiation into new territory, and what is behind us is bid farewell. Similarly, with each conscious turn, our minds open up for the planting of new seeds and release of old patterns derived from trauma.

Grief is a responsibility of the aging, a gift to be bestowed upon the young. We who allow ourselves to "do grief" show those following in our footsteps that they can, too. To be modern is to see many things that our recent ancestors could not. To look further back is to borrow from the ancient ones and recover what has gotten lost amid industrial hustle and modernization.

You can learn by looking back into your ancestry that death was not always such a sterile event. A select portion of my people's people, the Bonepickers, were those who facilitated ceremonial preparations of and for the deceased. While their methods would be considered rather gruesome by modern standards, I hear their message loud and clear: Tend Your Dead.

By honoring grief, you revitalize what many want to turn away from: the beautiful and timeless human process of being fully present with the real-time sorrow of loss.

Decay is what feeds new life. To pivot from death and seek higher ground is to miss out on a critical aspect of life. We have become too overprotective of what is real and inescapable. The wounds must be cleaned until they heal.

The dearly, and even not so dearly, departed will not have peace until they are honored and remembered. So must it be with the smaller deaths and dissociations that occur inside of our lives on this side of the grave.

ACKNOWLEDGEMENTS

I am utterly grateful for the endless support for Prayers of Honoring from those who are working to heal prayer trauma and develop their conversational ways with the Mystery as they understand it.

It is an honor to be able to lay these words out on the world altar. Thank you for finding ways to utilize the prayers in unconventional situations and surprising settings.

I owe profound gratitudes to Heather Dakota, Henry Cordes, Natalie Gildersleeve, Elena Brower, Stephanie Ladd, Jen Gray, Christine Mason Miller, Stefanie Lindeen, Twozdai Hulse, Annie Adamson, Tanya Hughes, Heaven McArthur, Holli Taylor, Irene Skau, Choctaw Nation of Oklahoma, and the brave students of Honoring Grief with Owl.

Honors to my dad, Donnie Carr, who makes room for my big feelings without taking them to the bank, though he was never trained to do so.

Thank you to my amazingly resilient brother, who has ridden some mighty waves and heals me with laughter and quick-wittedness.

Deep and humble gratitude to grief guerrilla Sky Sharp, for his unwavering love and support and for walking his healing talk.

Lifelong appreciations to Miles Lighthorse and Ivy Tallulah for their willingness to explore all of the avenues of your pain with me when I am the cause of it and when I am not.

Carr writes as Pixie Lighthorse to honor her indigenous ancestors of the Long Walk. As an enrolled member of the Choctaw Nation of Oklahoma, she is the author of the Prayers of Honoring Series, Boundaries & Protection, and Goldmining the Shadows.

Lighthorse received her training in transformational shamanism between 2003-2012. She was born in California amidst farms, ranches, animals, and wildlife and holds a degree in fine art and literature. Feminine and earth-centered sensibilities for the cornerstone of her work.

66606161R00074

Made in the USA
Columbia, SC
22 July 2019